Making miracles with my mindset

Verses Kindler Publication

VERSES KINDLER PUBLICATION

Verses Kindler Publication.

Website: www.verseskindlerpublication.com

Making miracles with my mindset

By: Ms. Shirley Singh

ISBN: 978-93-5605-973-3

FICTION STORIES 1st Edition

Price: $12

<u>Disclaimer</u>

Making miracles with my mindset is written by Shirley Singh.

The published work is the original contents of the author and she has done her best to edit and make it plagiarism free.

The characters may be fictitious or based on real events but they are not meant to hurt anyone's feeling nor portray anything against any caste or system.

In case of any plagiarized write-up the author is solely responsible for it, the publisher would not be responsible for it.

Foreword:

This book is my story, but it does not just belong to me.

It is an expression of immense gratitude to all those who have been a part of my journey and given me the courage to see it through. It is also a heartfelt appeal to all those battling with health problems to never give up on yourself. I hope that even in the darkest of days, my story can be a guiding light for you towards strength and positivity.

Chapter 1:

In our young age, we often daydream and envision how our future life will be. We get inspired by all the good things we see around us and try to incorporate those in our imagination of the kind of people we will become, the lifestyle we lead, and the values we hold close to our hearts. I was no different, and I used to picture an ideal and perfect life for myself. The picture had no traces of the relentless battles that would be waged against me by my own body. That being said, it also did not have traces of me turning into an unstoppable force. We never picture scenarios that have our determination, willpower, and resilience pushed to new thresholds. But these were destined for me, and I am thankful for the invaluable lessons they taught me and how they moulded me.

I was born among the hustle and bustle of New Delhi and brought up in the serene and peaceful town of Mombasa, Kenya. The fondest memories of my childhood are the carefree times I spent with my friends. Our ritual for every weekend used to be to get together at my house, since I had a squash court and swimming pool. We would spend hours swimming, and playing squash, French elastic, and hide & seek. For my parents, I was the apple of their eye. The immense love they showered on me while I was growing up has shaped my personality in more ways than I can express. I lived a completely sheltered and protected life where no problems or troubles were allowed to make their way to me. As comfortable as I was in this cocoon, I knew that someday I would need to leave it and face the real world. That time came for me when I decided to leave my parents and my home and venture to a college in the land of dreams, Mumbai. I was a model student and sincerely attended every lecture since my biggest desire was to make my parents proud. Life in this fast-moving city felt like a sharp contrast from what I was used to. I learned some of these new ways, but I was fortunately spared from the many challenging housing and food problems that most students face in a new place. I lived with my aunt, and like my parents, she took very good care of me.

Out of nowhere, I started having trouble breathing. My chest used to feel like it was closing up at times, and I used to be deeply gasping for breath. I was told that it was asthma and that I would need to rely on an inhaler henceforth. As a girl of 20, this worried and scared me for I did not know how I would be able to cope with it, but I eventually did. My asthma as good as vanished a few years after this point, and I rarely needed an inhaler. My family soon found an eligible suitor for me. Before I had time to fully process this enormous change, we were engaged and were to be wed soon after my college ended. It was not my choice as I wanted some more time to develop myself and explore new avenues, but I never expressed my thoughts. I knew my parents would only want the best for me, and so I decided to take the leap of faith. Within a month after my engagement, a cascade of problems descended on me. My eyesight deteriorated and had to wear glasses. My skin, which I had always maintained well, had relentless breakouts of acne. And to top it all, my digestive system gave me trouble due to which pain and bloating became unwanted constants in my life. I was struggling to find my footing in this trying phase, when I had another blow dealt to me. A mere few weeks before the marriage, our engagement was called off. I was never told the reason, and that sent me down a rabbit hole of anxious thoughts. I felt like I had set out to make my parents proud but had somehow done the polar opposite. My parents were, like always, the biggest source of encouragement for me and my aunt too immensely helped me tide through that difficult period.

After having gained much perspective over the years, I can now say it was perhaps a blessing in disguise because that was not the person I saw or wanted as my life partner.

I had always heard that good things were in store for those who have faith. I believed that a kind and compassionate man was waiting for me, but little had I expected to meet him and become his fiancé within a few weeks after my engagement broke. We were married in 1995. We enjoyed the newlywed bliss and I spent most of my time with my husband and family. I thought that I was expected to dress conservatively and thus wore only salwar kurtas. It was my mother-in-law who told me that my thinking was wrong and that I should not hesitate to wear western clothes. I felt very accepted and liberated. During that time, I had a first-hand experience of the power that our thoughts wield and came to realize that all illness stems from our mind. As suddenly as my eyesight had worsened, it was completely cured. I got rid of my glasses, and I bid them a permanent adieu, so much so that I have never needed them to date. I also took a step toward entrepreneurship after my marriage and started selling homemade chocolates and cheesecakes to a store in Pune. I was offered the chance to supply my products to a popular restaurant in the city, but it never materialized because we were expecting a joyous addition to our family.

In 1998 & 1999, we were blessed with two baby boys. This phase was as difficult as it was beautiful. My firstborn was 2 months premature, and the delivery triggered severe backache problems. I needed support to even get out of bed, and that's when I turned to yoga. The asanas worked magic on my muscles and eradicated my pain in 8 months. My second born was more than 2 months premature. I spent 3 nights alone at the hospital while my boys were in the NICU. I had insomnia and severe anxiety creep up on me, but I didn't have the luxury to mentally crumble or give up. They needed me, and my maternal instincts were fully geared to keeping myself aside and thinking about them. I kept my problems at bay, toughened up, and developed mental tenacity. I believe that yoga also contributed to me finding my composure and remaining calm in the face of crisis. The shedding of pregnancy weight, which is challenging for many, happened in the most natural way for me. Since I was up and about immediately after both my deliveries, I did not have to struggle to get my body into shape. My high activity levels achieved that for me. I resumed my small business and took it a step further by starting my own cooking classes. I had a routine of doing yoga thrice a week till the birth of my second son and this consistency in exercise had a holistic positive impact on my health. However, my motherhood duties took precedence then, and I wanted to devote any free time that I had to my kids and family. I took a break from it then, and resumed yoga again after 10 years which was the best gift that I could give myself. It improved my physical and mental well-being and helped me realize the enormous preventative and curative benefits that come with regular exercise.

Chapter 2:

I was extremely content with my roles as a mother, wife, and businesswoman. I was not searching for anything more in life, but the things that are meant for you will always find their way to you. 2 years after my second son was born, our prayer group was hosting a function and I volunteered to choreograph and perform a dance with some kids. It was a big success and I had mothers urging me to start dance classes. I leaped at the chance, and it brought me immense joy. My first batch had 8 girls and I had set up a dance show for them. I invited my son's primary school principal for it too, and the show ended with me having a job offer in hand! I joined the school as a 'tot a robics' teacher and taught and performed dances and sports drills with small children. Another surprise avenue opened for me when I participated in a beauty pageant upon my friends' insistence. At 33, I was competing against 18-year-olds, but I won it. The judge there had opened his own gym, and through a friend's recommendation, he agreed to take me on as a trainer despite having no certification. I took high-intensity sessions that combined many dance forms with aerobics. I got settled into my new routines and used to happily look forward to every new day.

However, little did I know that I had something else in store for me. It started off with some bleeding irregularities during my menstrual cycle. I tried to wait it out for whether it would resolve itself, but I ended up having to undergo 2 cervix biopsies within 3 years. The results were negative, but the gynaecologist forewarned me that I would develop cancer down the line, for I had all the symptoms of it. I was merely 36 years old at this time and the news devastated me. I thought that the life I had dreamt of for myself was being snatched away from me. Later though I realized that by worrying myself about something that may or may not happen in the future, I was denying myself the chance to fully live in the present. I took on 'que sera, sera' as my mantra and decided to face that situation if and when it came.

Months rolled by and I was blissfully living in the world of my work and family life. But that dynamic would change soon as I tore my ACL ligament. A big part of my daily routine and a big source of my happiness seemed in jeopardy since my doctor initially advised me to undergo surgery and stop all classes. The thought of giving up everything that I had worked for pained me infinitely more than the injury. I insisted and pleaded with the doctor for an alternative. He suggested an option that not many people agreed to, but I was determined to see it through. I started doing ankle weights 4 times a day with 3kg weights. It was excruciating but completely worth all the pain as I was able to resume my school classes in just 2 weeks. I used to limp up 3 flights of stairs and teach kids with the help of other teachers. I did the standing actions, but they performed the jumping and squatting actions as per my instructions. I would not have been able to do it without their support. It took me 6 weeks to regain the ability to conduct my gym sessions. I could not perform the vigorous jumping actions like before, but I could manage the dance movements by putting more pressure on my uninjured leg. Against all advice, I chose not to take painkillers at the time so that I would know exactly how much pressure I could exert without aggravating my knee. I also did an additional set of ankle weight exercises before and after the classes. The complete recovery, which took over 10 years, demanded a lot of time and patience, but I learned that powering through is the only way out. The Universe loves to tease and test stubborn people, and it rewards the ones who succeed in its tests by not giving up.

Sometime shortly after that, I remember waking up one night with a painful cough. I tried the typical remedies that we've all been told of, but warm water, gargles, or even hot turmeric milk stood no chance against it. The cough eventually started a negative domino effect of sore throat and inflammation. I got a diagnosis of bronchitis from a doctor and started a dose of antibiotics. I had to repeat another round, which took away my most of my energy but not my ailment. It had reached a point where my doctor advised me to get admitted because I could collapse at any moment, but I had a strong gut feeling against it. I felt that getting admitted would not be the solution, and thus I decided to consult another doctor. He recommended I take an allergy test, and the results were such that robbed me of every joy I had in life. I discovered that I was severely allergic to almonds, cashews, yeast, soy, and flowers, and these were the things that I had surrounded myself with on a daily basis. Bread was one of my favourite items; I had toast for breakfast and a doughnut with my evening tea almost every day and indulged in pizza every week. I loved seeing the bright colours and taking in the pleasant fragrance of flowers, and thus I had them all over my house. My daily habit of eating dry fruits too had to change, and my only solace was that I could continue eating chocolate for dessert after lunch and dinner. But my joy was very short-lived, for I realized that chocolate contains soy. I was angry and frustrated at the situation, but those feelings dissipated once I realized that giving up these things was taking me a step closer to good health. I switched from bread to healthy parathas for breakfast and had pizzas with millet bases. People are only now beginning to see the extraordinary benefits of a millet-rich diet that helped me in so many ways. It healed my gut over time, and I have now restarted eating almonds and cashews. I treat myself to a little chocolate too now and then, but the daily cravings that I used to have for it have gone.

Like most women out there, I too am conscious and concerned about having a good figure. A slender waist is the ultimate beauty characteristic that's perpetuated by our society's mindset and media, and I always wanted to maintain myself. After I switched out bread from my diet, I realized it was one of the biggest impediments to gaining a fit and lean body. I realized that losing weight involves no rocket science and that people unnecessarily overcomplicate it. I never had to resort to extreme diets or measure and count every bite that I ate. Simple but impactful changes like avoiding maida, bread, deep- fried foods, and refined sugar can make all the difference. Instead of abusing my body with harsh food restrictions, I learned to respect it and provide it with wholesome meals. I urge everyone to treat their body like a temple for only then will you be able to see its unfiltered and beautiful side.

Chapter 3

2012 saw many theories, predictions, and wild conjectures floating around about the arrival of Doomsday. There were extensive articles written, and movies made on how the world, as we knew it, was due to end that year. By God's grace, this did not hold true for the greater masses. For me, however, 2012 did drastically change my life. To call it a difficult period would be a gross understatement. That year threatened to take away everything from me, and its immense and compelling force made me feel like giving up in some instances. I often felt powerless, like I was a weightless leaf being thrown around by harsh and unforgiving winds. I desperately wanted to regain control over my mind and body, but it felt akin to gripping sand in a closed fist- the harder you hold on, the more sand is going to slip out of your grip. But as we know, every coin has two sides. Every new trial and tribulation that I faced became the building block of a steel armor that strengthened me and made me undefeatable. After surviving what I endured and emerging unscathed from that experience, I truly believe I can overcome any curveball that life throws my way.

A grave prediction regarding my future had been made after my cervix biopsies. Since worrying incessantly about it was not going to help, I had made a conscious decision not to sit mulling over it. I moved on to better and more exciting things and pushed this monster deeper and deeper into my closet. It was dormant for a while, but it had not been vanquished. It was only a matter of time before it reared its ugly head and struck, and that happened in 2012. I was diagnosed with cancer. I was told to undergo a uterus removal surgery, and I was in such shock from what was happening to me that I could not fully comprehend what I was being told to do. I let the advice of the doctor wash over my ears and a decision in favor of the procedure was made. I was sitting by myself the night before the scheduled surgery, trying to introspect and prepare myself for what was due to happen. To date, I cannot explain what happened to me then; it may have been divine intervention or an overwhelmingly fierce gut feeling, but I opted out of the surgery. I confided only in God and trusted that he would ensure I was making the right choice. I subsequently consulted roughly 8 other doctors, all of whom told me that the surgery was the only available option. I kept taking multiple second opinions, till I eventually found Dr. Manisha Joshi. I was transparent about my expectations from her; that I was firmly against the surgery because I believed that emotional support and holistic well-being would help me. She upheld her belief that the surgery was advisable, but she was extremely loving, supportive, and patient with me.

The signs of the immense struggle I was going through showed on my body. I lost 7kgs within a month and everywhere I went, people inquired if I was sick. I made an excuse about being overworked and feigned a smile while I felt intense despair internally. I did not want my family to see me breaking down, so I used to fabricate having plans with friends and instead used to sit alone and sob for hours in the car.

Here is a mantra I followed, 'I nourish my mind with positive energy. I let go of thoughts that drain me and refocus myself on thoughts that empower me.'

I continued taking classes because they served as a good distraction, but even there I avoided mingling with people and started making excuses to avoid all social plans. The classes became increasingly taxing on my body, coupled with the fact that my ligament injury had not fully healed. I decided to shut down my dance academy in which I had invested 13 years of my life, but I kept up the school and gym classes. Shortly after, I discovered to my horror that I had started coughing up blood. I was terrified to be told that something else had transpired in my body and hence chose not to consult a doctor. I dealt with this roughly for 2 months, but there were other relentless problems coming my way. My upper arms became covered with painful, pus-filled acne and I developed eczema.

I had 2 routes in front of me then. I could succumb and be defeated in this war against my health, or I could transform into a fierce warrior and fight back with everything that I had. The former seemed like the easiest thing to do, but I am grateful to have found the courage to choose the latter. I started researching about cancer and identified the small changes I could make in my lifestyle that could have a big impact. I turned to meditation which helped me find calm amidst all the chaos in my body and mind. I started by doing it for very small intervals, but even that helped me so much that the practice has stuck with me to date. I changed my diet and became vegan for almost a year. I had also read that oxygen kills cancer cells. I used to gasp out loud for air whenever I used to cry, and I continued with my high-intensity cardio classes, both of which contributed to an increased oxygen intake. The culmination of all these practices and changes made the impossible possible. My health was still in poor condition, and I still displayed the symptoms, but the test conducted after roughly 6 months was negative for cancer. With small steps and large amounts of willpower, I kept up this positive trajectory. When I met Dr. Joshi a year later, my uterus looked healthy again. Hearing her say those words overwhelmed me with relief. I had almost agreed to a major surgical procedure that would have altered my body's physiology, and my decision to not do it had scared me many times. I used to wonder whether I was making a mistake that could cost me my life. I thanked my stars that I could see my decision through, despite all doubts, and that I was dearly rewarded for it. Dr. Joshi also told me that I would perhaps reach the stage of menopause very late in life. The lifestyle changes that I had temporarily adopted became a permanent switch, which made me feel mentally and physically healthy. At 51, I have still not experienced menopause.

Along with Dr. Joshi, Dr. Dave too really helped my recovery. He is a renowned doctor from Mombasa who was, luckily for me, in Pune at that time. He wasn't practicing but he met me since he was well-acquainted with my parents. He told me that I looked fine and advised me to hang in there. His words gave me tremendous hope, and I realized that a lot of battles are first fought within your mind. If you can fight your demons then and there, you have a much better chance of conquering everything else. I realized that my ill health was the most evident on my face and body when my mind wasn't healthy. I am a living testament to how the right mindset can see you through the toughest of times. It is also extremely important to treat your body preciously and only give it as much nutritious food as you can. The importance of this cannot be stated enough. I have come to believe the saying that we are what we eat, and having a healthy approach towards food will reflect in a healthy mind and body.

Chapter 4

After the storm of the year 2012 had passed, and I had saved my life from being completely uprooted and destroyed by it, some semblance of normalcy returned to my world, but my fears were far from alleviated. I smiled and put on a pretense of enjoying myself with my family and friends, but despair and anxiety had a firm hold over me. I tried to find solace in and reignite my passion for my work. I tried to keep up the highly beneficial lifestyle changes that I had adopted through the myriad of health problems that I had suffered because they had done so much more for me than simply help cure the problems; they had carved the path for me toward a richer and fuller life, and I wanted to continue treading it. It took a while to overcome the lasting effects of the time I had endured, and I used to initially be paranoid about everything that I ate out of the terror of my health problems resurfacing. But time eventually healed my wounds, and I had acquired a more grateful outlook towards everything that I had been blessed with. The next 2-3 years went by so, but their end ushered in the beginning of a new era in my life.

I was in the midst of my class one day when I felt a strange growth on my abdomen. I powered through the class, but upon examining it closely at home, I realized that there was an apparent lump. We rushed to consult a doctor and were informed that it was an abdominal hernia. Even before the doctor said it out loud, I had braced myself to hear that I would need to undergo surgery. It felt like déjà vu. I had, once before, gone against medical advice, held off on a surgery, and it had been for the best. I had no way of knowing whether things would pan out the same way again, but I felt I owed my body a chance to heal without being cut into. I kept pushing through in this condition for almost a year, till one fine day the pain reached an intolerable level. I could not move or even stand straight without curling up in agony, and that's when my family put their foot down. They insisted on the procedure, and it was scheduled for a week later. The pain had blocked out most of the events leading up to it, and the next thing I remember is awakening in a hospital room after the surgery. I knew that my family had taken the right call and that whatever happened had been for my benefit. I had easily accepted that my body would bear scars from the surgery, but I was in for a big surprise when the surgeon, Dr. Pradeep Sharma, eventually opened the dressing.

He had done such an exceptional job that even a single scar could not be seen. I was pleasantly surprised and asked about how this happened, and that's when he told me that he had been extra careful to not leave marks because I had a lovely and well-maintained stomach. I was delighted with the outcome, yet I thought that the scars would not have mattered to me since I was almost 45 years old at the time and rarely wore clothes that exposed my midriff. But down the line, I realized that I had shied away or simply never considered doing so many things because it was not socially common. I made the doctor's efforts pay off and started freely and frequently wearing crop tops and sports bras after the age of 50. To date, I thank him in my mind whenever I wear short clothes because I feel free and do not need to be conscious about how my body looks. The recovery too after the surgery did not take long; certain breathing problems persisted, and I had been told to avoid ab exercises, but I could resume my school classes after 2 weeks and gym classes after a month.

In the meanwhile, the problems of eczema and acne that I had contracted shortly after the cancer had still not subsided. It had also taken a toll on my hair, and I had started experiencing extreme hair fall. I had tried every possible remedy; I did antibiotic courses prescribed by skin specialists, used the leading haircare oil brands, and even tried regular facials, but nothing worked. I decided that I had had enough and went on a complete detox. I stopped using all commercial products skincare and haircare products, and even went off makeup. I decided to turn to natural ingredients that have been tried and tested over time and make my products using them. I devoted a lot of time to research and eventually identified the building blocks that I could use to formulate my own body butter, facial moisturizer, serum, face and body wash, hair wash products, and healing oils. Next came the challenge of finding the right proportions to incorporate the ingredients. I tried various permutations and combinations, and I was the guinea pig for each of these experiments. Doing so helped me get to the crux of the problem with each of my product versions. I exactly knew when the body butter was too thick or thin. This helped enhance my understanding of the products and now I know the exact proportions that should be used and how even the weather influences these ratios. I started using only my range of products and relied on other traditional remedies that I had read about like Epsom salt and neem juice. I feel that my body was craving this natural touch because after I made the switch, my eczema never returned, the hair fall drastically reduced, and my skin had never looked as flawless. I met one of my previous students many years later, and one of the first things she asked me was the treatment that I was taking for my skin since it looked so good. When I told another person who I met sometime later that the secret of my healthy skin was my own products, she told me that I could be a real-life, walking & talking advertisement for them. Her words got me thinking, and I ultimately got the confidence to share my products with more people since I had personally experienced their benefits. I started gifting them to my students, and soon enough I got such a good response that I started selling them solely through word-of-mouth marketing.

My newfound knowledge about these long-forgotten healing techniques not just helped me, but my family too. My son developed a large and painful corn on his foot and was told to get it surgically removed. I asked him to hold off on it for just one month, and I used to keep his feet soaked in Epsom salt and warm water while he studied. It did the trick, and his corn completely vanished within 3 weeks. In 2018, I got a brief chance to restart my dance classes that I had been forced to shut down due to my deteriorating health. 8 of the young girls that I used to teach came back to learn from me. I was excited to venture once again on this journey. For almost 2 years, I taught them dance aerobics and even shared health & body care tips with them, but this came to a stop just before the lockdown. During that same period, there came a day when I was overcome with a sudden shooting pain in my heel. It was an inflammation condition called plantar fasciitis. My large toe also developed a painful infection, which made it turn almost black in color. And to top it all, bunions too started forming on my feet. I didn't quit on my classes; since my shoes covered my feet, I kept going like normal but would return home and keep my feet soaked in Epsom salt. I was told that I may not be able to wear heels in the future, but I refused to accept that. I started sunbathing every morning and did exercises specially targeted for toes and feet. I was thankful that this coincided with the period of lockdown since all my classes had stopped and I could devote time to exercising and sunbathing. My toe healed naturally, the foot pain and bunions vanished, and the high heels that I comfortably wear make me feel beautiful and confident to take on anything that comes in my path!

Chapter 5

The year 2020 is etched deep into every person's mind. It was a time when fear and despair had taken over. The lockdown, which was for our safety, was a very troubling time for many people who could not cope with the solitary lifestyle and the ceasing of all social activities. I consider myself extremely privileged that my story for 2020 was different than this, and that it turned out to be one of the best years of my life. After the never-ending struggles with my health and the responsibility of managing those while keeping up my work and family life, I was forced to take a step back and just slow down. It helped me align and center my life, which had gone askew due to the constant pressures that pulled at me from various directions. I rekindled my love for dancing and started calling my students over to my house where we used to dance our hearts out, make fun videos, and post them to YouTube. We weren't doing it to get attention or for the views; we did it for ourselves and so it didn't matter even if people thought it was frivolous. I also rescued 3 kittens during that time and absolutely loved the feeling of being a cat-parent. That year really helped me to see the world and my life through a new and brighter lens.

Unknown to me, plans for the next battle that my body was waging against me were perhaps already in motion. It took me a while to see the tangible signs of it, and the first instance was sometime in the middle of 2021. I was enjoying a relaxed evening at home when my neck seized up in pain, as did the entire left side of my body. I attributed it to physical fatigue and there were no warning bells ringing for me. However, within an hour or two, I felt my heart beat unnaturally fast and I could not talk properly or move my neck. I was aware that if my family knew the full extent of what was happening, they would pressure me to get admitted, which I absolutely wanted to avoid. The palpitations showed no signs of stopping, and I spent the entire night doing pranayama lying down since I could not sit. It worked its magic after a few hours and the palpitations were under control. Till the next morning, the pain too had disappeared. The potential and importance of pranayama cannot be emphasized enough, and I truly wish to spread more awareness about its power so that more people and enrich their lives with it. The second instance came in October 2021. When I first opened my eyes, it seemed like any normal day, but very soon trouble signs started ringing in my head when I became aware of my entire body being in agonizing pain. I panicked and tried to get up, hoping that I would be able to make sense of what was happening to me. Instead, I made things worse and immediately collapsed. This situation was a mystery for every doctor that we consulted; my reports were all clear and there was no evident diagnosis, but the fact remained that something was drastically wrong with my body. One doctor and physiotherapist eventually told me that despite the negative report, it looked like a case of rheumatoid arthritis. They were as surprised by this as I was, given how active I kept myself and the other good lifestyle practices that I had. I took it in my stride and encouraged myself to fight this obstacle too like I had done with all the others. Painkillers were to become a constant in my life, but I took matters into my own hands. I refused to live on daily medication, and it made a big impact on my life. The same things that earlier used to take me 10 minutes to complete started taking me an hour, and simple tasks like walking or even holding a plate became very increasingly difficult. Seeing my condition, my husband advised me to quit my job at the school, but I convinced him that I could manage since they were online classes. I smartly modified my teaching style in a way that my inability to move properly was not evident and yet it remained enjoyable for the children. The weeks dragged by painfully, but the positive outcome was that I knew my resilience was limitless. It was this staunch belief in myself that kept me going. An opportunity for me to push myself to a new level presented itself in December 2021, when I got an order for 200 homemade soaps that were required to be made in just 5 days. My condition at the time was such that even chopping up vegetables had become a strenuous task. My family stepped up then and became my helping hands. My husband, both sons, and even their girlfriends worked with me to complete the order, and we managed to do it in just 4 days. The client gave me exceptional feedback, but what made me even happier was that I had not lost my drive and the guts to take on things even when circumstances were difficult.

The system that I had in place with my school classes was going better than I expected. Nobody who saw me in actual life then could imagine that I was conducting online dance sessions, but I was handling it well. This status quo was to change soon though since the school decided to go offline in February 2022. I had to drive myself to school and it took me the strength of both my hands to simply change gears. Additionally, I had to lug a heavy speaker up to there which seemed completely beyond my physical capacity. I had been given an intimation of this one week prior by the school, and I fully utilized that time to mentally prepare myself for what I needed to do. The obvious solution, which even my husband urged me to consider was to resign, but instead, I tried to mentally strengthen myself with meditation and gain more control over my body. I eventually resorted to a painkiller before my first day and that helped ease the pain. It was still extremely difficult, however, the sense of accomplishment that I got after every class made it all seem worth the efforts I was making. The joy of taking and putting up videos of my dancing that I experienced during the lockdown kept me wanting for more. My physical constraints did not allow me to do full videos, so I turned to making short reels. Shooting a reel of merely 30 seconds demanded a recovery time of almost an hour, and nobody could understand why I was so determined to continue doing it. Candidly speaking, even I wasn't sure what the reason was, but something in me was telling me to keep going. I even shot a very creative dancing reel in a swimming pool that was comparatively easier to do since I couldn't feel as much pain in the water. In June 2022, I joined a gym upon my kids' insistence. I spotted a monkey bar on my second day there and made up my mind to complete it before my 50th birthday.

My trainer, Roopa, was my support system. I started off with barely being able to hold onto the 1st rung for 2 seconds, and when I tested myself 2 days before my birthday, I could go till the 4th rung. The day finally arrived, and I just decided to go all out without being held back by self-doubt. I told Roopa to shoot the reel and I started on it; to my extreme delight, I did not stop till I had completed it! I felt immensely proud of myself and was excited about where my fitness journey would lead me.

Unfortunately, I had a setback planned for me. Merely 3 days after this achievement, I had a bad fall on a staircase while I was leaving for my class. I iced my back where the full impact of the fall came, waited for the shakiness that I was feeling to dissipate, and then went to school. It was there that I realized my back was bleeding and swollen. I spent that entire day in crushing pain and was later told by the doctor that I narrowly escaped a very severe spinal fracture. I took complete rest for 5 days before bouncing back to conduct my classes, and 10 days before rejoining the gym, though my injury had only recovered partially. I took it upon myself to strengthen my back and worked religiously toward it in the gym. I could notice the differences within a month and felt internally stronger. The only other reminder of that fall existed in the form of the wound marks that it left, but I knew a sure-shot remedy. I concocted a product that I used daily, and the marks faded away within a year, leaving me a clean slate upon which I could write new chronicles of good health, fitness, and well-being.

Chapter 6

Through gym, I had found a new passion in life that challenged, motivated, and excited me. I kept learning more about my body and developed a deeper understanding of exercises. I felt my body was getting stronger and healthier, but this state was set to change soon. I was overcome by extreme jaw pain that gave me no indication and suddenly one day thrust itself upon me. Before I knew it, it had progressed to the stage where talking became a painful proposition and my diet had to only comprise of soft foods or things could be finely ground. I knew I desperately needed medical help, but all my past memories with doctors were haunting me and I felt too emotionally drained and tired to put myself through it again. I also didn't know a doctor who could help me in that case, and so, I decided to help myself. I did in-depth research and discovered some jaw exercises. It took every bit of mental strength I had to keep these up, since they were so painful, but my perseverance eventually produced results. The constant pain that I felt subsided over a few months; though it periodically recured even after that, the intensity was much lesser. When I rejoined the gym after my back injury, I took baby steps and worked out with minimal weights. I was content with doing that temporarily and was eagerly awaiting the time when I could scale to new heights of training, but little did I know that there was something else in store for me. I discovered that I had started bleeding every time I attempted lower body or abs exercises, and hence I stopped doing them. However, I continued going to the gym and that's where I found a muse for the next fitness activity I wanted to take on. I saw a young girl hanging from a bar, doing a backward summersault, and effortlessly landing on her feet. I was amazed and got fixated with the idea of doing the same. I was not in a good shape at the time due to the bleeding, and poor upper body strength; but I still requested the girl to show me how to do it, spent all my time in the gym that day practicing it, and managed to do it on the 1st day itself! When the 2nd day came, I slipped and had a fall, and I was extremely scared since there was no cushioning. I froze in fear and was unable to shake this off for almost 2 weeks. Every time I tried, I could only take my legs up to the bar and did not have the guts to take the next step. And yet, I felt haunted about abandoning it and the desire to accomplish it eventually overpowered my fear. I successfully attempted, and within a week after that, I shot a beautiful reel wherein I timed my summersault and landing to the beats of the music.

It was at this point that I realized the highly empowering effect that creating these reels had on me. They became a source of motivation for me because I found myself willingly testing my limits, and in the process, regaining my mental and physical strength. To survive reality sometimes we need fantasy, and that's what my reels are for me. I can blissfully get transported to a la-la land for a few hours every day just by thinking about and planning the reels. I also fulfilled my dream of having a bikini photoshoot done at the age of 51. My efforts towards working on my handstand paid off; a few days before the shoot, I managed to spring up my legs against a wall, which I had previously struggled with, and thus I used that too as a pose for my photoshoot, with the addition of high heels. I was so confident in my decision and so proud to openly embrace the body that I'd worked hard to build, that I did not let any inhibitions or worries about what people would say come in my way. I was fiercely driven to keep trying new things and continued practicing hanging backward summersaults, and even headstands. I was just about getting in the groove of acing these new things when a shoulder injury slowed me down. I refused to let go of the progress I'd worked towards and chose to continue going to the gym. I did lightweight shoulder exercises and banded exercises to enhance strength. Since I had taken a long break from leg workouts, I thought I could restart them without triggering the bleeding problem, but my assumption could not have been farther from the reality. I started bleeding from the very day that I started lower body exercises, but I ended up ignoring it. This cost me dearly, and eventually, the bleeding became so profuse that even tablets could not get it under control. The first doctor whom I consulted advised me for a uterus removal procedure, and I turned instead to an ayurvedic doctor, Dr. Vivek Jadhav. He gave me some medicines that helped me to a certain extent. Simultaneously, my yoga instructor, Dipesh Sancheti curated my exercises to improve pelvic strength. I also kept focussing on good nutrition and daily breathing exercises, and ultimately, all these aspects came together to benefit me.

My shoulder took its own sweet time to recover, and 8 months went by in this process. It used to immensely bother me that all my work towards perfecting the hanging summersaults and handstand would be lost due to this setback. Inspiration to overcome this struck me one day when I saw a reel of a girl doing a handstand and getting into a car. I knew I wanted to do that and was willing to go to any lengths for it. My son came to stand by me for the first attempt, but I could not do it. I still remember his words when he went up to my husband and said that I had zero strength in my body, but I had a mind of steel. They were both worried that I would injure myself further and pleaded with me to let go of it. I heard them out, but I could not get myself to do it. I asked Roopa to help me with it the next day, and that attempt too was unsuccessful. All my practicalities were telling me to move on from it, however, my fierce desire to recreate that reel eventually triumphed over them. I tried once again and I managed to do it, though I was very unsteady and needed to grab onto the side mirror and window ledge. I decided to take the leap and planned to shoot the reel the next day after this, and I even surprised myself when I did it perfectly in one go! My shoulder pain aggravated slightly, but I could barely notice it over the sheer jubilation and exhilaration that I felt in every pore of my body.

Chapter 7

I was floating on cloud 9 till many days later. The fact that I could create a great reel was among one of the reasons, but far from the only. I was the happiest at discovering a new version of myself. A version that was fierce, unwavering in her dedication, and willing to move mountains to achieve anything she set her mind on. It changed the way I perceived myself, and I could see pride and awe shine out for me from my family's eyes. I felt like I had earned the right to be my sons' role model. There had been several challenging moments in their lives too, and they never shied away from telling me how much I had influenced and motivated them. I could also touch a few more lives, which made every victory of mine much sweeter since I had people to share it with. After seeing my bikini photos, one of my former clients and friend, Diviya, reached out to me to help her with her fitness. I told her I had no training, but she insisted since she had firsthand seen a transformation in me. I chalked out a nutritious diet plan and exercise routine for her that included all the things I was doing at home. She stuck with it, and within 9 months had lost 9 inches each from her chest, hips, and abdomen. She had been unsuccessful in losing weight for 30 years, and I was ecstatic to have been able to give her a healthier life. I was also lucky to receive love and admiration from my growing social media family. I largely owe this book to someone who gave me the much-needed push to share my story. A person who had seen my reels suggested that I pen down my fitness journey, since I could inspire and help people. The idea had captured my imagination, but for the longest time, I did not act on it. This person continuously motivated me and nudged me toward it after seeing a few more of my reels, and gave me the faith that my story should be shared since it can benefit many others. I am glad to have found such an unexpected source of encouragement.

My gym conducts annual fitness events. Back in 2022, I had tried running in the competition, but I had barely done 200 m when an agonizing pain shot through my head up to my neck on one side of my body. My jaw too had jammed up and my face had turned ice cold. This bad experience had unnerved me, and made me request my trainer that for the 2023 competition, I would do anything besides running. However, the format this time included teams, and fate made it so that everyone refused to run. I did not want to let the entire team down, so I agreed to the race. On my first attempt at practicing for it, my jaw pain returned with a vengeance and my face went cold. My leader was extremely supportive, but I never told him about my problem because I knew he would advise me to not strain myself. I desperately wanted to come through for my team and test my limits in the process. I had one practice with my leader and the team, and later, I started going by myself at 5:30am since I did not get time during the day. I started off needing 4 mins to complete a round, but my consistency came to my aid, and on the day of the competition, I did it in 2 min 40 seconds and won a gold and bronze for my team. I achieved this despite having pulled a muscle near my hip just 5 days before the race. That had been a highly challenging week for me since both my sons had been injured in unfortunate accidents. I had spent every waking moment taking care of them while juggling the household chores and my training. I could never have foreseen at that time that me and my sons overcame all odds and performed well in the competitions that we participated in. They later said to me, "You never give up in any situation, so how could we?" and the knowledge that I have helped them become stronger and resilient will keep me going through everything else that life throws at me. I believed more than ever at that point that a strong mind can commandeer you toward every victory you wish to earn. I also picked up new hobbies that I enjoy doing, such as karaoke. I tried it on a whim in June 2023, but it helped me in more ways than one. I thoroughly enjoyed myself while doing it, but miraculously, my jaw pain that used to continually persist would vanish a day or so prior to karaoke and I could sing pain-free! The highlight of that year however would be the 5km marathon that I did successfully and easily on 31st December. I was once at a stage where even standing and walking used to take a toll on me when I was told I potentially had arthritis, and I had suffered a ligament tear too in the past. Completing the marathon was the most befitting kind of New Year celebration for my body, and I was excited to venture into 2024 to grow and heal some more.

In the next month, I took up a wedding choreography after almost a 12-year hiatus from it, and the first session ended with an intense attack of jaw pain. I happened to visit my dentist the next day, and I returned home with a reinforced belief in cosmic powers. My usual dentist happened to be unavailable, and I requested the receptionist for a consult with any other available dentist there. She sent me to a jaw surgeon, who provided an answer for some of the mysteries my health had posed over the years. I was diagnosed with degenerative joint disease and osteoarthritis. The inexplicable jaw pain and the crippling body aches that I suffered from in 2020 suddenly made sense to me now. The surgeon advised me to get a jaw replacement surgery. When she asked me how and why I thought of consulting her, I truthfully told her that I believed God had directed me to her doorstep. I took a second opinion which corroborated the diagnosis; the other doctor told me that my joint was sliding out of place whenever I opened my mouth and shifting back in when I shut it. At last, I understood the reason for the pain I was enduring. I am thankful that I started jaw exercises when I did, for their timely impact really saved me. I was unwilling to undergo the procedure, and hence the doctor prescribed me some more exercises with higher repetitions. I have complete faith in myself that I will win this battle too and emerge stronger than ever from it. I cannot put into words the exact feeling I had when I knew what lay ahead of me. Fear was nowhere on the horizon; I was, in a way, excited to take on and vanquish a new demon because I felt something good would come out of it and I would overcome it.

In addition to the enhanced jaw ache, I started experiencing pain in my shoulders, wrists, and knees every morning. It used to remain so for the entire day, but I found a magic cure for it, although temporary, in the gym. Exercises started relieving much of the pain and my evenings became considerably better. Strength training truly helped me, and I started setting myself harder challenges in the gym and my dance classes. It takes a lot to overcome them, but I am getting there, slowly but surely. In the meantime, my bleeding problem was nowhere close to subsiding. Till February 2024, it had worsened to a point where I barely had one week free of bleeding in the whole month. Within 3 days after I had gotten the diagnosis, I took it upon myself to accomplish a 45kg deadlift, which would be the maximum weight I had ever tried. Since the bleeding was triggered by leg and abdominal exercises and a deadlift entailed both, I had barely practiced it for several months. The heaviest that I had been able to lift was a single repetition with 38kg. However, I had my eyes on a target, and nothing would shake my resolve. I kept going, and I initially succeeded in lifting the weight for 5 repetitions, but my form was wrong. I continued doing more till I eventually got it right! And the most astonishing part was that my bleeding had somehow, completely stopped.

As my story draws to a close, I want the good parts to be remembered, but I know in my heart that I would not have got a chance to experience them if I did not get a taste of the bad. I experienced severe depression for almost a decade; a plastered smile for others and lonely tears for myself marked those 10 long years of my life from 2012-2022. I want to open myself up completely to everyone who revisits my journey through the pages of this book, and I can accept here that I contemplated putting a brutal end to it all at one point. I wrongfully convinced myself that life was not worth living, but God and the memories of my loving family brought me back from that dangerous point. I share this in the hopes of resonating with such feelings that may develop in others, and to convince you that there is always a silver lining to life that you just need to find. I found mine through my spirituality, fitness, nutrition, mental strength, pursuing things that I love, and being with people whom I love. And last but not the least, by learning to love myself and appreciating everything that I have gone through and emerged unscathed from. The renowned book 'Laws of the Spirit World' was a true eye-opener for me and gave me a deeper perspective on life and living. I realized that there was a world of difference between being alive and living. I imbibed all these new learnings, and the dawn of 2023 turned me into the biggest fan of who I am and what I stand for. I await each new day with electrifying energy coursing through my body to do more, learn more, and be a better version of myself than I was the day before. This is my mantra to keep living, and shining on for the days to come!

Note for the reader –

Kindly consult a doctor in case of any medical emergencies.

Verses Kindler Publication

Reach us through our website -

https://www.verseskindlerpublication.com/

For more information visit our Instagram or Facebook page.